D0579710

P7-CGZ-470

SandCastle™

Perfect Pets

Hidden Hermit Crabs

Kelly Doudna
AUTHOR

C.A. Nobens
ILLUSTRATOR

Consulting Editor, Diane Craig, M.A./Reading Specialist

ABDO
Publishing Company

Published by ABDO Publishing Company, 4940 Viking Drive, Edina, Minnesota 55435.

Printed in the United States.

CREDITS

Edited by: Pam Price

Concept Development: Nancy Tuminelly

Cover and Interior Design and Production: Mighty Media

Photo Credits: Anders Hanson, Connie Johnson, Kellie Puddy, Coral L. Saunto, ShutterStock

LIBRARY OF CONGRESS CATALOGING-IN-PUBLICATION DATA

Doudna, Kelly, 1963-
  Hidden hermit crabs / Kelly Doudna ; illustrated by C.A. Nobens.
     p. cm. -- (Perfect pets)
  ISBN-13: 978-1-59928-751-5
  ISBN-10: 1-59928-751-X
  1. Hermit crabs as pets--Juvenile literature. I. Nobens, C. A., ill. II. Title.

SF459.H47D68 2007
639'.67--dc22

                    2006034582

SandCastle™ books are created by a professional team of educators, reading specialists, and content developers around five essential components—phonemic awareness, phonics, vocabulary, text comprehension, and fluency—to assist young readers as they develop reading skills and strategies and increase their general knowledge. All books are written, reviewed, and leveled for guided reading, early reading intervention, and Accelerated Reader® programs for use in shared, guided, and independent reading and writing activities to support a balanced approach to literacy instruction.

SandCastle Level: Transitional

LET US KNOW

SandCastle would like to hear your stories about reading this book. What is your favorite page? Was there something hard that you needed help with? Share the ups and downs of learning to read. We want to hear from you! To get posted on the ABDO Publishing Company Web site, send us e-mail at:

sandcastle@abdopublishing.com

HERMIT CRABS

Hermit crabs are shy and spend a lot of time hidden in their shells. But they come out to climb, eat, and change shells, which is fun to see.

Dominic feeds his hermit crab fruit, vegetables, and meat. Today it is eating carrots, lettuce, and blueberries.

Lillian makes sure her hermit crab has water to drink and swim in.

As it grows, a hermit crab needs to move into a bigger shell. Bryce gives his hermit crabs several shells to choose from.

Jada puts rocks, branches, and rope in the tank for her hermit crabs to climb on. Hermit crabs are very good climbers.

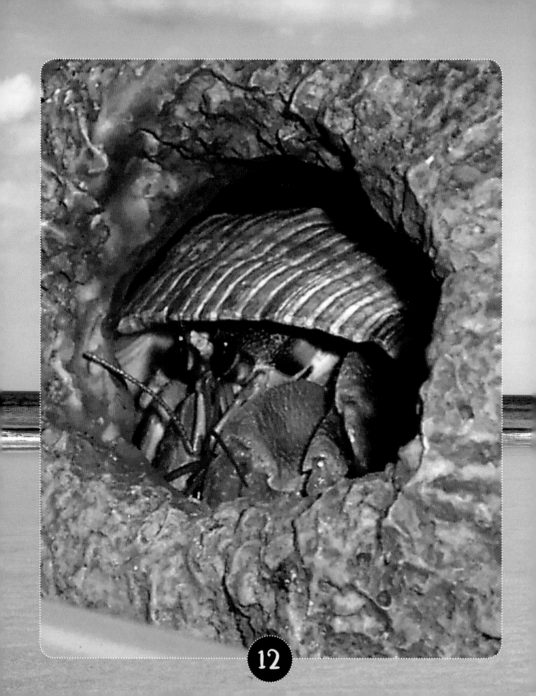

Carter's tank has a cave.
His hermit crabs can hide
inside it and feel safe.

A Hermit Crab Story

Hermin the hermit crab hides all day. Hannah wishes he'd come out and play.

Hannah gives Hermin
a new empty shell.
She hopes he'll like it.
Time will tell.

To Hermin, the new shell
looks more roomy.
He moves into it
and isn't so gloomy.

Hermin parades his new shell around his aquarium. Hannah is pleased at how happy he's become!

Fun facts

If you have more than one hermit crab, you can start a "shell cascade." Place an empty shell in the habitat. After the first crab leaves its old shell, the other crabs will all change shells too.

Although it is not ideal, hermit crabs will use things other than seashells for their homes. A hermit crab will use a bottle cap, an empty can, or anything else it can find that suits its need.

A hermit crab will molt several times during its lifetime. When it is time to molt, the hermit crab will burrow under the sand and stay there until it is ready to shed its old exoskeleton. This could take days or weeks.

Glossary

choose – to pick one of two or more options.

empty – having nothing inside.

fruit – the fleshy, sweet part of a tree or plant that contains one or more seeds.

gloomy – feeling sad and hopeless.

tank – a large container for fish or reptiles to live in.

vegetable – the edible part of a plant grown for food.

About SandCastle™

A professional team of educators, reading specialists, and content developers created the SandCastle™ series to support young readers as they develop reading skills and strategies and increase their general knowledge. The SandCastle™ series has four levels that correspond to early literacy development in young children. The levels are provided to help teachers and parents select appropriate books for young readers.

Emerging Readers
(no flags)

Beginning Readers
(1 flag)

Transitional Readers
(2 flags)

Fluent Readers
(3 flags)

These levels are meant only as a guide. All levels are subject to change.

To see a complete list of SandCastle™ books and other nonfiction titles from ABDO Publishing Company, visit **www.abdopublishing.com** or contact us at: 4940 Viking Drive, Edina, Minnesota 55435 • 1-800-800-1312 • fax: 1-952-831-1632